Bergen's Best Bridge Tips

D0062406

By Marty Bergen

Bergen Books

Thanks To:

Layout, cover design, and editing by
Hammond Graphics.

My very special thanks to: Cheryl Angel, Cheryl Bergen,
Trish and John L. Block, Ollie Burno, Jim Canty,
Pete Filandro, Jim Garnher, Terry Gerber,
Lynn and Steve Gerhard, Steve Jones, Doris Katz,
Danny Kleinman, Harriet and David Morris,
Phyllis Nicholson, Mary and Richard Oshlag,
Helene Pittler, Sally and Dave Porter, David Pollard,
Mark Raphaelson, Jesse Reisman, Carl Ritner, John Rudy,
Maggie Sparrow, Merle Stetser, Bobby Stinebaugh.
and Bob Varty.

Bergen Books
9 River Chase Terrace
Palm Beach Gardens, FL 33418-6817

First Printing: April 2004
Second Printing: August 2006

Library of Congress Control Number: 2004092321

ISBN: 0-974471410

Dedication

In memory of my father,
Jack Bergen.

A good man who
loved his family very much

BRIDGE BOOKS BY MARTY BERGEN

More Declarer Play the Bergen Way

Bergen for the Defense

Declarer Play the Bergen Way

Bergen's Best Bridge Quizzes, Vol. 1

To Open, or Not to Open

Better Rebidding with Bergen

Hand Evaluation: Points, Schmoints!

Understanding 1NT Forcing

Marty Sez

Marty Sez...Volume 2

Marty Sez...Volume 3

POINTS SCHMOINTS!

More POINTS SCHMOINTS!

Introduction to Negative Doubles

Negative Doubles

Better Bidding with Bergen, Volume I

Better Bidding with Bergen, Volume II

FYI

The player with the bidding decision to make is indicated by three question marks: ???

For consistency, South is always that player, and his hand is the one displayed.

Every bidding diagram begins with West.

West	North	East	South
—	—	—	2♡
All Pass			

The dashes are place holders, and in the example above, show that the auction did not begin with West, North, or East. The dealer was South.

The "—" does not indicate a "Pass."

**For information on ordering books
and interactive CDs from Marty,
or taking a Bridge Cruise,
please refer to pages 69 - 72.
GREAT DISCOUNTS!**

**To order, call
1-800-386-7432**
or email: mbergen@mindspring.com

CONTENTS

Appendix

Stop – Read This

Bergen's Best Bridge Tips (BBBT) is a continuation of my *Bergen's Best Bridge Quizzes* series. Each book will feature tips and quizzes based on an assortment of practical topics.

Each chapter will deal with a specific auction and provide 10 hands for you to decide what to bid. I urge you to think about each hand as if you were actually "at the table," and to write down your action before reading on.

In addition to the bidding quizzes, each chapter contains a separate quiz on card-play. Four of these non-bidding quizzes deal with declarer play, while the quiz in chapter 5 focuses on defense. Each of these card-play quizzes consists of several questions, which are then answered in detail.

I've tried to explain my answers as thoroughly and helpfully as possible. If you like, you can grade yourself by awarding 10 points for each correct answer. Of course, you may decide that you are right and I am wrong, and that you got 100 while I only scored 60%. Fair enough!

Stop - Read This

Although everyone loves to get good grades, how you scored is not the key. All that matters is what you know *afterwards,* and how you apply what you've learned when you play bridge.

Does it matter if you're playing matchpoint duplicate, team of four, or rubber bridge? **Not at all.** I recommend every bid, play, and lead described in this book regardless of the form of scoring.

Do not overlook pages 62 - 68. The two segments provide valuable information along with page numbers to allow you to easily locate the pages where they origionally appeared.

I.   Bergenisms
These concise, carefully-worded statements can be an invaluable aid to the reader in countless situations.

II.   Glossary Plus
For your convenience, a listing and explanation of conventions and terms used in BBBT that may not be familiar to all players.

Opening Bids as Dealer

(relevant to chapter 1)

Five-card majors.

Using the Rule of 20, we may open light (subject to good hand evaluation) in first or second seat.

1NT opening bid = 15-17 HCP.
2NT opening bid = 20-21 HCP.

2♣ opening bid is strong, artificial, and forcing.

Weak two-bids in diamonds, hearts, and spades.

Rule of 20 – What's the Story?

Why is the Rule of 20 so helpful?
It provides an easy but accurate method to determine if your hand is worth an opening bid.

When do you apply it?
In first or second seat, when unsure whether or not to open a borderline hand. It is not relevant in third or fourth seat.

What do you do?
Add the length of your two longest suits to your HCP.

What then?
If the total is 20 or more, open the bidding.
Use your normal criteria in deciding which suit to bid.
With fewer than 20, unless your hand qualifies for a preempt, you should pass.

It will be very helpful to count your quick tricks.
Here is a review of this important topic.

For each suit:

AK = 2,   AQ = 1½,   A = 1,   KQ = 1,   Kx = ½

Jacks are never "quick," and the maximum number
of quick tricks per suit is 2.

How many quick tricks do you need to open?
Most hands worth an opening bid have at least
2 quick tricks. But, no hard and fast rule is possible.
Some hands with 1-1½ quick tricks should be opened.

You are the dealer with both sides vulnerable.
Evaluate each hand and decide what to do.

1. ♠ Q 5   ♡ A K 4   ◇ J 7 5 3   ♣ Q 6 5 4

2. ♠ A J 10 8   ♡ 7 5   ◇ A Q 10 9   ♣ 6 5 3

3. ♠ K Q   ♡ Q J 5   ◇ K Q J 7   ♣ J 7 6 5

4. ♠ K 10   ♡ A 8   ◇ K Q 6 5   ♣ K 10 6 5 3

5. ♠ Q J 7   ♡ K J 5   ◇ A K Q   ♣ Q 7 5 4

6. ♠ A 6   ♡ K 9 7   ◇ K 10 3   ♣ A Q J 10 8

7. ♠ —   ♡ A J 10 9 7   ◇ A 8 6 5 4 2   ♣ 6 3

8. ♠ A 10 9   ♡ A K 9   ◇ 7 6   ♣ A K Q 10 5

9. ♠ J 5   ♡ 6 5 4 2   ◇ A K J 9 8 2   ♣ Q

10. ♠ A K Q J 8 7 5   ♡ A 6 5   ◇ A 2   ♣ 7

You are the dealer with both sides vulnerable.

1. ♠ Q 5   ♡ A K 4   ◇ J 7 5 3   ♣ Q 6 5 4
Which minor should you open? Neither! You should
pass. On the surface, you satisfy the Rule of 20
(12 HCP + 4 diamonds + 4 clubs = 20), and you do
have 2 quick tricks. However, your holdings in
spades, diamonds, and clubs are not worth their
point count. **Be wary of hands with more queens
and jacks than aces and kings, and hands which
lack intermediates.**

2. ♠ A J 10 8   ♡ 7 5   ◇ A Q 10 9   ♣ 6 5 3
Open 1◇. You might think of this as a balanced hand
with 11 HCP which doesn't satisfy the Rule of 20
and choose to pass. But, as far as I'm concerned,
I love the way the aces, honors, and intermediates are
concentrated in the two longest suits. Also, the
majority of hands containing 2½ quick tricks are
worth an opening bid.

3. ♠ K Q   ♡ Q J 5   ◇ K Q J 7   ♣ J 7 6 5
Yuck! Open 1◇, rather than 1NT. This mess is not
worth anywhere near 15 HCP! You have six quacks
(queens and jacks), no aces or intermediates, and KQ
doubleton is not worth 5 HCP. In addition, opening
1NT with only 2 quick tricks is extremely rare.

4. ♠ K 10   ♡ A 8   ◇ K Q 6 5   ♣ K 10 6 5 3
Open 1NT, as opposed to 1♣ or 1◇. Despite the two
doubletons, the advantages of 1NT far outweigh the
disadvantages. 1NT immediately defines your
strength and avoids potential rebid problems.

5. ♠ Q J 7   ♡ K J 5   ◇ A K Q   ♣ Q 7 5 4
Open 1NT! Although you have 18 HCP, this is
definitely a "not worth its point count" hand. You have
4-3-3-3 distribution and *not one* intermediate card.
2½ quick tricks is a horrible number for a hand with
18 HCP. This over-rated hand is nothing more than a
stronger version of the very *ugly* hand #3.

6. ♠ A 6   ♡ K 9 7   ◇ K 10 3   ♣ A Q J 10 8
Open 1♣. Vive la différence! Without question, this
is a " too good to open 1NT" hand. You have 3½
quick tricks, several intermediates, a lovely 5-card
suit, and your only quacks are in your long suit.
You're quite willing to jump to 2NT at your next turn.

7. ♠ —   ♡ A J 10 9 7   ◇ A 8 6 5 4 2   ♣ 6 3
Open 1♡. You have *a lot* of offense and adequate
defense. Whether or not you use the Rule of 20,
(9 HCP + 6 diamonds + 5 hearts = 20), this should
definitely strike you as a hand that you don't want to
pass. You won't pick up many 6-5 hands, so make the
most of every one of them. By opening 1♡, you'll be
able to show both your suits without reversing.

You are the dealer with both sides vulnerable.

8.　♠ A 10 9　♡ A K 9　♢ 7 6　♣ A K Q 10 5

Open 2♣, intending to rebid 2NT, promising a balanced hand with 22-23 HCP (or an unattractive 24). Some would say that all you have is a balanced hand with 20 HCP. **Marty Sez:** with 5 quick tricks and promising intermediates, *and* a likelihood of 8 playing tricks, this hand is too strong to open 2NT. I also believe that three aces are worth more than 12 HCP.

9.　♠ J 5　♡ 6 5 4 2　♢ A K J 9 8 2　♣ Q

Open 2♢. In my mind, this is a sensible compromise between 1♢ and pass. Here are my thoughts:

I do open *light*, but the honors in the short suits are *very* questionable, so I wouldn't open 1♢. Although some players regard it as sacrilege, preempting with a very weak 4-card major on the side doesn't bother me a bit. As for pass, I'd certainly hate to miss an opportunity to show off these pretty diamonds.

10.　♠ A K Q J 8 7 5　♡ A 6 5　♢ A 2　♣ 7

Open 2♣, not 1♠. With 4 quick tricks and 9 playing tricks, you satisfy all of the requirements for a 2♣ opening bid. The fact that you have only 18 HCP should not deter you. If you open 1♠ and everyone passes, you'll be sick to your stomach.

14

North

Contract: 4♡
Lead: ♡2
Both sides vul

♠ 4
♡ K Q J 8
♢ A 10 7 5 3 2
♣ Q 10

South (You)
♠ A Q 8 7 6
♡ A 10 9 5
♢ —
♣ 7 6 5 3

West	North	East	South
—	—	—	1♠
Pass	2♢	Pass	2♡
Pass	4♡	All Pass	

You open your light but attractive hand based on the 2½ quick tricks, diamond void, and major-suit intermediates.

You end up in 4♡, but are not thrilled to receive a trump lead. You win with dummy's ♡J, cash the ♢A and discard your ♣3.

Question 1: After West's annoying trump lead, how many sure winners do you have?

Question 2: What's your best chance for a 10th trick?

Question 1: After West's annoying trump lead, how many sure winners do you have?

Answer: Only nine. If you crossruff diamonds and spades with the six remaining trumps, you would fall one trick short. Because two of your side's trumps had to be played at the first trick, you'd be limited to a total of seven trump winners and two aces.

Question 2: What's your best chance for a 10th trick?

Answer: You need to win the ♠Q. You lead dummy's ♠4 and East plays low. Although dummy has only a singleton, you should finesse the ♠Q.

As long as West doesn't have the ♠K, you're looking good. Cash the ♠A, and discard a diamond or club from dummy. You're now ice-cold. You've won four tricks, and still have three high trumps in each hand. Crossruffing spades and diamonds will result in your making 10 tricks.

On the other hand, if West has the ♠K, your goose is cooked. He will lead another trump, and you might even go down two. C'est la vie!

Postscript: As you can see on the next page, the ♠K was right where you wanted it to be. Your good technique was rewarded and you scored up 4♡.

Making the First Move

Here is the entire deal:

Contract: 4♡
Lead: ♡2
Both sides vul

North
♠ 4
♡ K Q J 8
◇ A 10 7 5 3 2
♣ Q 10

West
♠ J 10 5
♡ 7 6 4 2
◇ 8 6
♣ A J 9 2

East
♠ K 9 3 2
♡ 3
◇ K Q J 9 4
♣ K 8 4

South
♠ A Q 8 7 6
♡ A 10 9 5
◇ —
♣ 7 6 5 3

West	North	East	South
—	—	—	1♠
Pass	2◇	Pass	2♡
Pass	4♡	All Pass	

AFTER YOU OPEN IN THIRD SEAT

On each of these hands, the auction has begun:

West	North	East	South
—	Pass	Pass	1 ◇
Pass	1 ♠	Pass	???

Keep in mind: Because partner is a passed hand, his response in a new suit is *not* forcing. Therefore, if you know that there is no game, it's up to you to end the auction ASAP without giving partner a chance to get you too high.

As South, evaluate each hand and decide what to do. The opponents are vulnerable; your side is not.

1. ♠ 8 3 2 ♡ A ◇ Q 7 6 5 4 ♣ A Q J 2

2. ♠ A Q 10 ♡ A ◇ 10 9 7 6 5 ♣ A 5 3 2

3. ♠ A 9 6 ♡ 8 6 3 ◇ A 8 7 3 ♣ A 6 3

4. ♠ J 7 5 2 ♡ K J 5 3 ◇ K Q J ♣ Q 4

5. ♠ K Q 9 7 ♡ 8 ◇ A J 8 5 3 ♣ 7 6 5

6. ♠ A 7 5 ♡ A K 10 ◇ A K 10 9 7 2 ♣ 6

7. ♠ A J 8 ♡ Q 3 ◇ K J 7 6 5 3 ♣ Q 5

8. ♠ 8 4 ♡ A Q ◇ A K 10 8 6 ♣ A 7 6 3

9. ♠ A K 10 8 ♡ A 6 2 ◇ A 10 9 7 4 ♣ 6

10. ♠ J ♡ A Q ◇ A K Q 9 8 7 5 ♣ 10 8 6

West	North	East	South
—	Pass	Pass	1◇
Pass	1♠	Pass	???

1. ♠ 8 3 2 ♡ A ◇ Q 7 6 5 4 ♣ A Q J 2

Pass. It would be easy to bid 2♣, but where are you going? With your mediocre hand, game becomes very unlikely once partner doesn't open. If partner had responded 1♡, you wouldn't dream of passing with a singleton, but playing in a 4-3 fit at a low level is okay.

2. ♠ A Q 10 ♡ A ◇ 10 9 7 6 5 ♣ A 5 3 2

Bid 2♠. With this stronger hand, you are not ready to give up on game. Your two possible bids are 2♣ and 2♠. With such good support for partner's major, a raise to 2♠ is a standout. **When in doubt, be eager to "support with support."**

3. ♠ A 9 6 ♡ 8 6 3 ◇ A 8 7 3 ♣ A 6 3

Pass. Although your distribution suggests notrump, you shouldn't bid 1NT. Why is that?

- With your flat 12-count, you have no interest in game opposite a passed hand. Don't give partner a chance to get you overboard.

- Having no stopper in the unbid major is a liability.

- Hands with aces play *very well* in suit contracts.

4.   ♠ J 7 5 2   ♡ K J 5 3   ◇ K Q J   ♣ Q 4

Pass! Yes, you are assured of a spade fit. But, with this aceless, spotless, ugly hand, you want no part of a spade game. Don't give partner *any* encouragement.

5.   ♠ K Q 9 7   ♡ 8   ◇ A J 8 5 3   ♣ 7 6 5

Bid 2♠. Partner's 1♠ response is music to your ears. This will be a lovely dummy in a spade contract, and you'll have no regrets if partner bids on.

6.   ♠ A 7 5   ♡ A K 10   ◇ A K 10 9 7 2   ♣ 6

Bid 2♡. A reverse into a 3-card suit is *not* pretty, but there is no alternative. This hand is far too good for an invitational 3◇ bid, and you're not ready to raise spades or bid notrump.

Don't be nervous. Because responder will go up the line with four cards in each major, if partner does raise your hearts, he guarantees five spades – so you'll be assured of a spade fit.

7.   ♠ A J 8   ♡ Q 3   ◇ K J 7 6 5 3   ♣ Q 5

Pass, instead of bidding 2◇. With a pair of Qx suits, this is another ugly hand which lacks game interest after partner was unable to open. 1♠ must be a playable contract, which may not be the case in 2◇. If you end up in 2◇ and partner has only a singleton trump, you could lose four trump tricks.

21

West	North	East	South
—	Pass	Pass	1◇
Pass	1♠	Pass	???

8. ♠ 8 4 ♡ A Q ◇ A K 10 8 6 ♣ A 7 6 3
Bid 2NT. The textbook rebid is 2♣, but 2NT is more descriptive. Where are the 18-19 HCP needed for this bid? If you love aces and long suits even half as much as I do, you would have upgraded this a point (or two).

9. ♠ A K 10 8 ♡ A 6 2 ◇ A 10 9 7 4 ♣ 6
Bid 4♠. With 15 HCP, 4-card spade support, and a singleton, you'd usually be content to invite game by jumping to 3♠. However, your 4 quick tricks and 3 trump honors call for a serious upgrade. If you play Splinter Bids, I do understand jumping to 4♣. But once partner limited his hand by passing, he'd need perfect cards for slam; and I learned the hard way never to play partner for perfect cards.

10. ♠ J ♡ A Q ◇ A K Q 9 8 7 5 ♣ 10 8 6
Bid 3NT. With 8½ tricks, this hand is much too strong for a non-forcing 3◇ bid, and any other bid would distort your hand. You'd like to have a club stopper, but it's far more likely that your opponents will lead the unbid major. **Opener's double jump to 3NT always shows a strong unbalanced hand with length and strength in the suit he opened.**

Contract: 2♣
Lead: ♣3
E-W vulnerable

North
♠ K Q 8 6 4
♡ 9 8 6 2
◇ 8
♣ 10 7 5

South
♠ 2
♡ J 5 3
◇ A J 7 6 3
♣ A K Q J

West	North	East	South
—	Pass	Pass	1◇
Pass	1♠	Pass	2♣
All Pass			

Question 1: What are your prospects for taking eight tricks?

Question 2: After winning the opening trump lead, what would you lead at trick two?

Question 1: What are your prospects for taking eight tricks?

Answer: You don't have enough fast entries to your hand to ruff several diamonds as well as setting up your fifth diamond. Therefore, you'll need to do something with dummy's spade honors. And you *must* work on that suit immediately. If you make the mistake of *first* playing the ◊A and ruffing a diamond on the board *before* playing spades, you'll be in trouble. When you then lead spades, the opponent will win his ♠A and lead a second trump, removing dummy's last trump. You won't be able to get to dummy, and will have no chance to win eight tricks.

Question 2: After winning the opening lead, what would you lead at trick two?

Answer: Lead your ♠2 and hope West has the ♠A. If he does, he has no good options. If he wins the ♠A and leads another trump, you can win and play the ◊A and ruff a diamond with dummy's last trump. You'll then be able to cash both the ♠K and the ♠Q.

If West ducks the ♠2, you will win dummy's ♠K. *Now*, you will be able to crossruff. You'll lead the ◊8 to your ace and ruff a diamond with the ♣7. You can then ruff a spade to your hand, and ruff another diamond with dummy's ♣10.

If East has the ♠A, you're going down. East will capture dummy's ♠K and lead a second round of trumps. You can cash the ◊A, ruff a diamond, and cash the ♠Q, but you'll still fall one trick short. Your only satisfaction will be in knowing that you played the hand correctly and gave yourself the best chance to make the contract.

Here is the entire deal:

North

Contract: 2♣
Lead: ♣3
E-W vulnerable

North
♠ K Q 8 6 4
♡ 9 8 6 2
◊ 8
♣ 10 7 5

West
♠ A 9 5
♡ K 7 4
◊ K Q 9 4 2
♣ 4 3

East
♠ J 10 7 3
♡ A Q 10
◊ 10 5
♣ 9 8 6 2

South
♠ 2
♡ J 5 3
◊ A J 7 6 3
♣ A K Q J

West	North	East	South
—	Pass	Pass	1◊
Pass	1♠	Pass	2♣
All Pass			

West	North	East	South (You)
—	1 ◇	Pass	1 ♠
Pass	2 ◇	Pass	???

Before considering your second bid, here is a quick review of what you know about North's hand.

The 2 ◇ rebid promises at least six diamonds. If opener has seven diamonds, he must have limited strength; otherwise he would make the invitational jump to 3 ◇. **On auctions like this, unless he has 100 honors, opener should not rebid a 5-card suit.** If he does, he could find himself in an absurd contract if you are forced to pass 2 ◇ with a weak hand and 0-1 diamond.

North should have a minimum opening bid, with less than 16 HCP. The only exception would be a fair hand with a suit that was too weak to jump to 3 ◇.

Opener's 2 ◇ rebid obviously denies 4-card support for spades. If opener has three good spades, he should often raise responder's major instead of rebidding his 6-card diamond suit.

Very important: Your holding in partner's long suit is *very* relevant. With a singleton or void, you should be pessimistic. However, with a fit for opener's suit, you can be optimistic. Any honor in opener's 6-card suit is worth its weight in gold.

After Opener Rebids His Minor

The next three pages describe your likely actions. Each category includes two examples. The first example is straightforward, while the second is less obvious.

West	North	East	South (You)
—	1 ◇	Pass	1 ♠
Pass	2 ◇	Pass	???

Pass: In addition to passing weak hands, you should be eager to pass with a fair hand that includes a misfit for diamonds.

♠ K 9 8 5　♡ K 5 3　◇ —　♣ J 8 7 6 5 3

♠ K Q J 4　♡ Q 6 5　◇ 6　♣ Q 7 5 4 2

2♡ : Forcing for one round, but not necessarily to game. Because you don't have many forcing bids available, you may have to make this cheap, forcing bid with three hearts.

♠ K Q 8 6 3　♡ A Q 10 7　◇ 3　♣ 7 5 4

♠ A K 9 7 5　♡ A 5 4　◇ A 6 4　♣ 9 2

2♠ : Shows a weak hand with a 6-card suit. If you have a misfit for diamonds, the hand might not be as weak.

♠ A Q 10 9 5 4　♡ Q 9 4 2　◇ 7 5　♣ 9

♠ K J 6 5 4 2　♡ K J 4　◇ —　♣ Q J 5 2

2NT: Invitational, usually with 10-11 HCP as well as stoppers in both unbid suits. You may or may not have a balanced hand.

♠ A J 7 4   ♡ K 6 3   ◇ J 3   ♣ Q 8 7 4

♠ K J 7 5 4   ♡ K 6 3   ◇ 6   ♣ K Q 7 4

3♣: Because you are going to a higher level, your new suit at the three level is forcing to game.

♠ K Q 7 5 4   ♡ 7 6   ◇ A 5   ♣ A J 9 8

♠ A 10 9 5 4   ♡ 7 6   ◇ K J 6   ♣ A Q 9

3◇: Invitational. Because you have a fit, you can have fewer HCP than for other invitations.

♠ J 9 8 2   ♡ 6 5   ◇ A 10 4   ♣ A 7 5 3

♠ 10 8 7 6 4   ♡ A   ◇ J 5   ♣ A J 8 5 3

3♡: There are several ways to play this bid, so a meeting of the minds is needed. Here are the possible interpretations, along with an example:

5-5 game-forcing

♠ A K 8 6 2   ♡ A Q 8 7 6   ◇ 10 4   ♣ 3

5-5 invitational

♠ K Q J 9 7   ♡ K Q 10 6 5   ◇ 2   ♣ 7 3

splinter raise – game-forcing

♠ K Q 9 7   ♡ 3   ◇ A 6 4 2   ♣ K J 4 3

3♠: Invitational to game with a strong 6-card suit and about 11 HCP.

♠ A Q J 5 4 2 ♡ A 4 ◊ 6 4 ♣ 8 5 2

♠ Q 10 8 7 5 4 2 ♡ K Q J ◊ K ♣ J 2

3NT: You needs a good hand with at least one stopper in both hearts and clubs. You are more likely to have four spades than five, because you are not giving opener a chance to show 3-card spade support. On this auction, opener will almost always pass 3NT.

♠ K 7 4 3 ♡ A 10 8 ◊ Q 7 ♣ A 9 5 3

♠ Q 9 6 4 ♡ K Q J ◊ K Q J ♣ Q J 3

4♣: This splinter raise of opener's suit suggests a diamond slam. You need a game-forcing hand with 0-1 club and at least three diamonds.

♠ K Q 7 5 2 ♡ A 9 8 ◊ K 9 8 7 ♣ 3

♠ A 10 8 7 5 ♡ J 7 3 ◊ A J 9 6 2 ♣ —

4♠: Shows an independent suit and a worthwhile hand, but virtually no interest in slam.

♠ A K J 10 8 7 5 3 ♡ J 6 ◊ 8 2 ♣ Q

♠ K Q J 9 8 6 5 ♡ Q 8 ◊ K ♣ K 7 5

After Opener Rebids His Minor

On each of these hands, the auction has begun:

West	North	East	South
—	1◇	Pass	1♠
Pass	2◇	Pass	???

As South, evaluate each hand and decide what to do. Only your side is vulnerable.

1. ♠ A 8 7 6   ♡ A 9   ◇ 4 3 2   ♣ Q 8 7 3

2. ♠ J 10 9 5   ♡ K 10 5   ◇ K 10 8 3   ♣ A 2

3. ♠ Q 9 6 4 3   ♡ K Q J   ◇ 6   ♣ Q J 5 3

4. ♠ K Q J 9 7 6 3   ♡ 4   ◇ 9 8 4   ♣ A 3

5. ♠ A K J 7 5 2   ♡ A J 10 2   ◇ Q 5   ♣ 8

6. ♠ A Q 3 2   ♡ A Q   ◇ J 7 6   ♣ 10 8 7 3

7. ♠ A J 10 9 5   ♡ A K J   ◇ Q 9   ♣ 7 5 4

8. ♠ J 7 6 5 3 2   ♡ 7   ◇ A 6   ♣ A 10 9 3

9. ♠ K Q 6 5 3   ♡ 9 7   ◇ 7   ♣ K Q J 9 6

10. ♠ K Q J 10 9   ♡ J 10 8 7 4   ◇ —   ♣ 8 5 4

After Opener Rebids His Minor

West	North	East	South
—	1♦	Pass	1♠
Pass	2♦	Pass	???

1. ♠ A 8 7 6 ♥ A 9 ♦ 4 3 2 ♣ Q 8 7 3

Bid 2NT. Although your diamonds lack quality, 3-card support for a 6-card suit is a huge plus, so you definitely have enough to invite a game in notrump. In addition, you love having two aces. **When you are hoping to make 3NT based on a long suit, but your side can't have 26 HCP, you need aces.**

2. ♠ J 10 9 5 ♥ K 10 5 ♦ K 10 8 3 ♣ A 2

Bid 3NT. With your magnificent diamond fit, sure stoppers, and some useful intermediates, you're far too strong to bid 2NT or 3♦. If partner has two red aces, you'll win 2 heart tricks, 6 diamonds, and 1 club. Obviously, North has more than 8 HCP.

3. ♠ Q 9 6 4 3 ♥ K Q J ♦ 6 ♣ Q J 5 3

Pass. You have a misfit for diamonds, a weak 5-card suit, no aces or intermediates, and a lot of quacks. You don't know if partner can make *eight* tricks with diamonds as trumps, but his chances must be better than your prospects of making eight or nine tricks without a trump suit. **There is a lot more to a good notrump contract than just having stoppers in every suit.**

4. ♠ K Q J 9 7 6 3 ♡ 4 ◇ 9 8 4 ♣ A 3

Bid 4♠. Even if partner is short in spades, this
certainly feels like your best contract. When opener
rebids diamonds, you have a much better hand than
if your red suits were reversed.

5. ♠ A K J 7 5 2 ♡ A J 10 2 ◇ Q 5 ♣ 8

Bid 2♡. With this very flexible hand, you have no
idea whether your side belongs in spades, hearts,
diamonds, or even notrump. In addition, slam is quite
possible. Opener's next bid will be helpful in deciding
where you should end up.

6. ♠ A Q 3 2 ♡ A Q ◇ J 7 6 ♣ 10 8 7 3

Bid an imperfect 3NT. You would be a lot happier if
you had a sure stopper in clubs. However, with your
balanced hand, any other bid would be a distortion.
If you're worried about the opponents being able to
take five club tricks – that is *very* unlikely. It is also
true that on this auction, the defender will often lead
the unbid major.

7. ♠ A J 10 9 5 ♡ A K J ◇ Q 9 ♣ 7 5 4

Bid 2♡. You are hoping to hear a spade or notrump
bid from partner. If he raises to 3♡, you will bid 3♠
and give him one more chance to bid notrump with a
club stopper (or two). If he happens to jump to 4♡,
you'll pass and hope to make 10 tricks in your 4-3 fit.

West	North	East	South
—	1♦	Pass	1♠
Pass	2♦	Pass	???

8. ♠ J 7 6 5 3 2 ♡ 7 ♦ A 6 ♣ A 10 9 3

Bid 3♦, to show an invitational hand with support. You are not strong enough to force with 3♣, and bidding 2♠ will land you in an inferior contract whenever partner is short in spades. If opener bids 3NT, I would expect him to make it.

9. ♠ K Q 6 5 3 ♡ 9 7 ♦ 7 ♣ K Q J 9 6

Pass. If you bid 3♣ and partner bids 3NT, you won't like your chances to make 3NT on a heart lead. There is an excellent chance that 2♦ is your last plus score. **When you smell a misfit, get out ASAP.**

10. ♠ K Q J 10 9 ♡ J 10 8 7 4 ♦ — ♣ 8 5 4

Bid 2♠. Although opener could have six diamonds and four hearts, this hand is not nearly strong enough for a forcing 2♡ bid. However, repeating your first suit is neither forcing nor even encouraging. Your spades are a guaranteed four tricks in a 2♠ contract, but are not worth much if diamonds are trump. Opener's hand is sure to be a better dummy for you than your hand would have been for him. **Any suit containing 100 honors can be treated as if it has an extra card.**

North

Contract: 3NT
Lead: ♠J
N–S vul

♠ A
♡ 7 6 4
◇ Q J 10 8 6 5 4
♣ A 10

South (You)
♠ Q 6 5 4 3
♡ K J 9
◇ A
♣ K Q 7 2

West	North	East	South
—	1◇	Pass	1♠
Pass	2◇	Pass	3NT
All Pass			

With a strong hand and weak spades, you didn't look for a 5-3 spade fit, but instead, jumped to 3NT.

You would have liked to develop diamonds, but West's spade lead knocked out a crucial entry to dummy. Unfortunately, without the diamonds, you have no chance to make nine tricks. You desperately need to find an entry to the board in addition to the ♣A.

Question 1: Is there a realistic hope of a 2nd entry?

Question 2: After you lead a diamond to your ace at trick two, what is your plan?

Question 1: Is there a realistic hope of a 2nd entry?

Answer: Yes, dummy's ♣10 provides a 50% chance of giving you the additional entry – that you *must have*.

Question 2: After you lead a diamond to your ace at trick two, what is your plan?

Answer: Lead a club, finesse dummy's ♣10 and say your favorite prayer. If West was dealt the ♣J, dummy's ♣10 will provide the additional entry that you need. You'll then drive out the ◇K and await developments.

Of course, even if the club finesse wins, you're not out of the woods yet. Although the ♣A remains as an entry to dummy's diamonds, you have no idea what will happen in the majors. Depending on the location of the opponents' honors in diamonds, hearts, and spades, you could end up with as many as 10 tricks, or as few as seven or eight.

Postcript:
On the actual hand, good news was followed by more good news.

First: and foremost, the ♣10 won. Yes!!

Second: When you then led dummy's ◇Q, you were pleased when West won the ◇Q. You were certainly not looking forward to East leading through your fragile major suits.

Third: Because East had no entries, the contract was no longer in jeopardy. What happened next? West defended well by exiting with a club. When you eventually came off dummy with a heart, West took the last three tricks with the ♡AQ and the ♠K. But with 6 diamond tricks, 2 clubs and 1 spade, you were delighted to score up your game.

Here is the entire deal:

North

Contract: 3NT

Lead: ♠J

N–S vul

♠ A
♡ 7 6 4
◇ Q J 10 8 6 5 4
♣ A 10

West		*East*
♠ K J 10 9 7		♠ 8 2
♡ A Q		♡ 10 8 5 3 2
◇ K 3 2		◇ 9 7
♣ J 6 4		♣ 9 8 5 3

South

♠ Q 6 5 4 3
♡ K J 9
◇ A
♣ K Q 7 2

West	*North*	*East*	*South*
—	1◇	Pass	1♠
Pass	2◇	Pass	3NT
All Pass			

West	North	East	South (You)
—	—	1◇	Dbl
Pass	1♠	Pass	???

North's nonjump response in a suit shows 0-8 points. If North had a better hand, he could either:

- jump to 2♠ (invitational) showing 9-11 points including distribution; or

- cue-bid 2◇, showing 12+ points; or

- jump to game with a long major suit and enough strength or shape to justify the bid.

After North's weak 1♠ response, you must proceed carefully, *even with an attractive hand.* What follows is a list of options for you as the doubler at your second turn. Each category includes two sample hands. The first represents a minimum for the bid, while the second shows a maximum.

Pass: This tells partner that your hand is limited. Your double could have been made with as few as 10 HCP (and good shape), but you also could have a strong hand with as many as 16 HCP. Even if you have 4-card support, you should pass whenever you believe that game is out of the question after partner's weak response.

♠ A 10 8 2   ♡ K Q 7 3   ◇ 8 5   ♣ Q 10 6
♠ Q 7 6   ♡ A K Q 4   ◇ A   ♣ J 7 6 4 3

Rebids by the Takeout Doubler

West	North	East	South (You)
—	—	1♢	Dbl
Pass	1♠	Pass	???

- After the minimum response, all bids promise extra values (17+ points).

- All raises promise at least 4-card support.

- All notrump bids should include at least one stopper in the opponent's suit.

- A new suit or notrump bid denies four cards in partner's major – and you might even have fewer than three with your big hand.

- Your only forcing bid is a cue-bid in opener's suit. Because other bids are not forcing, they are all limited in strength.

1NT: Promises a hand too strong to overcall 1NT at your first turn, so double followed by a bid of 1NT shows 19-20 HCP.

> ♠ A 6 3 ♡ K Q J ♢ A K 6 ♣ Q 9 7 3
> ♠ K J 4 ♡ A Q 8 6 ♢ K 9 ♣ A K 7 5

2♣: A bid in a new suit shows a good 5-card suit (at least) and may include the unbid major.

> ♠ A Q ♡ K J 8 4 ♢ 6 3 ♣ A K 7 4 2
> ♠ A J 5 ♡ K Q ♢ J 4 ♣ A K J 8 6 5

2♦: This cue-bid shows a terrific hand, usually 19+ HCP. It is forcing for one round, and has no upper limit. You may have 4-card support, or you might have a big hand with 2-3 spades.

♠ A Q 2 ♡ A K 10 ♦ 8 6 4 ♣ K Q J 8
♠ A K ♡ A K Q 6 ♦ 8 5 ♣ A K J 8 7

2♡: Promises at least a strong 5-card suit.

♠ A 9 5 ♡ A Q J 10 4 ♦ A 5 ♣ Q 7 6
♠ A K ♡ K J 8 6 5 4 ♦ J 9 5 ♣ A K

2♠: The single raise shows 17-20 points, including distribution, as well as 4-card support.

♠ K Q 7 5 ♡ A 8 4 ♦ 9 7 ♣ A K 9 8
♠ A Q 6 4 ♡ A Q J 5 ♦ 8 4 ♣ K Q J

2NT: 21-22 HCP; does not deny 4 hearts.

♠ A Q 7 ♡ K J 3 ♦ A J 7 ♣ A Q 6 3
♠ K Q 8 ♡ A K 7 3 ♦ A K ♣ K 10 8 6

3♣: This invitational jump promises *great overall strength* and at least a strong 6-card suit.

♠ A J ♡ A J 9 ♦ K 6 ♣ K Q J 10 9 2
♠ K Q 7 ♡ A K 3 ♦ J ♣ A Q J 9 8 6

3♡: The same requirements as 3♣.

♠ K Q J ♡ A Q 10 9 6 5 ♦ 8 ♣ K Q 3
♠ A 7 3 ♡ A K Q J 9 8 ♦ 7 ♣ A J 3

3♠: This very strong raise will often include 5-card support. With 4-card support and similar strength, you might prefer to cue-bid at your second turn, to stay low if partner is broke.

    ♠ K Q J 6 3   ♡ A J 9 7   ◇ 7   ♣ A J 7
    ♠ A Q 7 6 4   ♡ A Q   ◇ K 5   ♣ K J 6 4

3NT: Insisting on game opposite a potential yarborough obviously promises a terrific hand, but not necessarily one that is balanced.

    ♠ J 6 4   ♡ A K Q   ◇ A K J   ♣ K Q J 9
    ♠ 5 3   ♡ A K Q   ◇ A Q   ♣ A K Q J 9 2

4◇: This splinter raise promises 0-1 diamond with at least four spades, and interest in slam if partner has a useful card (or two).

    ♠ A K Q 7   ♡ A Q J   ◇ 7   ♣ K Q 8 6 4
    ♠ A K 7 5 4   ♡ A Q 6 4   ◇ —   ♣ A Q J 7

4♡: Shows an independent suit with an excellent chance for 10 tricks in your own hand.

    ♠ A K 10   ♡ K Q J 9 8 7 2   ◇ 3   ♣ K Q
    ♠ A 7   ♡ A K Q 9 7 5 3 2   ◇ A 3   ♣ 7

4♠: You need very little help from partner to make game in his suit.

    ♠ A K 10 7 6   ♡ K Q J 7   ◇ A K   ♣ 8 4
    ♠ K Q J 9 6 4   ♡ A K Q J   ◇ K J   ♣ Q

Rebids by the Takeout Doubler

On each of these hands, the auction has begun:

West	North	East	South
—	—	1♦	Dbl
Pass	1♠	Pass	???

North's 1♠ bid shows 0-8 points. If he had more, he would have jumped or cue-bid.

As South, evaluate each hand and decide what to do. Neither side is vulnerable.

1. ♠ A 6 ♡ A 9 8 5 ◇ A Q 9 ♣ A 10 5 3

2. ♠ Q 7 6 4 ♡ A J 6 ◇ K Q ♣ Q J 8 5

3. ♠ A Q 3 ♡ 8 6 4 2 ◇ A 10 ♣ K Q J 8

4. ♠ A 9 ♡ A Q J 7 5 ◇ K 5 ♣ K 10 8 3

5. ♠ A J ♡ K Q 4 ◇ 9 6 ♣ A K Q 8 5 2

6. ♠ A J 9 8 ♡ K Q J ◇ Q 3 ♣ K Q J 4

7. ♠ A Q ♡ A Q 7 5 ◇ K Q 4 ♣ A J 5 3

8. ♠ A K Q 10 9 ♡ K J 4 ◇ A 6 ♣ Q J 9

9. ♠ A 10 9 7 5 ♡ A K 10 8 ◇ 3 ♣ A Q 9

10. ♠ K Q 6 ♡ A K J 4 ◇ 5 3 ♣ A K J 5

West	North	East	South
—	—	1♢	Dbl
Pass	1♠	Pass	???

1.   ♠ A 6   ♡ A 9 8 5   ♢ A Q 9   ♣ A 10 5 3

Bid 1NT. You correctly decided that your four aces and promising diamond holding made this hand too strong for an immediate 1NT overcall (15-18 HCP). This upgradable hand is worth at least 19 points in a notrump contract.

2.   ♠ Q 7 6 4   ♡ A J 6   ♢ K Q   ♣ Q J 8 5

Pass. You do have 4-card support, but with this ugly hand, where are you going? If all partner needed for game was a hand like this, he would have bid more than 1♠. You have too many queens and jacks, and too few aces and kings. In addition, KQ doubleton in the opponent's suit is definitely *not* worth 5 HCP.

3.   ♠ A Q 3   ♡ 8 6 4 2   ♢ A 10   ♣ K Q J 8

Pass, again, although *this* hand is not ugly. It would not have been wrong to overcall 1NT initially, but at this point, your 16 HCP are not enough to rebid 1NT (which would show 19-20). In fact, you don't have any good bid. Once you have doubled, you should not raise with only 3-card support. You promised support for all unbid suits, so when partner bids your 3-card suit it should be viewed as a disappointment.

4. ♠ A 9 ♡ A Q J 7 5 ◇ K 5 ♣ K 10 8 3

Bid 2♡. Doubling and then bidding your own suit promises at least 17 points. Your 2♡ bid shows 5-6 hearts and, obviously, fewer than four spades.

5. ♠ A J ♡ K Q 4 ◇ 9 6 ♣ A K Q 8 5 2

Bid 3♣. With this powerhouse, a "double and bid your own suit" scenario is not enough. Your jump is not forcing, but is *highly* invitational. You don't need much from partner to make 3NT.

6. ♠ A J 9 8 ♡ K Q J ◇ Q 3 ♣ K Q J 4

Bid 2♠. Remember that partner has not promised any strength. When he fails to jump, he can't have a decent hand, so you must proceed carefully. Despite your 19 HCP, you have too many queens and jacks to justify a stronger bid than a single raise. To have *any* chance for game, you'd need to find partner with two significant honors – and even that may not be enough.

7. ♠ A Q ♡ A Q 7 5 ◇ K Q 4 ♣ A J 5 3

Bid 2NT to invite game. Should I be worried that partner will not know how strong I am and we'll miss game? Not at all. Because a 1NT rebid after a double shows 19-20 HCP, it is logical that a jump to 2NT shows more than that. Personally, I'm more concerned that, if partner has nothing, even 2NT will be too high.

West	North	East	South
—	—	1◇	Dbl
Pass	1♠	Pass	???

8.　♠ A K Q 10 9　♡ K J 4　◇ A 6　♣ Q J 9
Bid 3♠. With your awesome trump support, it is tempting to jump to 4♠. However, you can't make a game all by yourself with this *balanced* hand. Getting to partner's hand may prove to be a huge problem. Content yourself with making a strong invitation.

9.　♠ A 10 9 7 5　♡ A K 10 8　◇ 3　♣ A Q 9
Bid 4♠. "Only" 17 HCP, but *now* you're ready to insist on game. On this auction, you'll have a more useful dummy than the previous example with the 20 HCP. You love the singleton and the wealth of intermediates. **When playing in a suit contract, the difference between 5-4-3-1 distribution and 5-3-3-2 is *very* significant.**

10.　♠ K Q 6　♡ A K J 4　◇ 5 3　♣ A K J 5
Bid 2◇. A cue-bid by the takeout doubler after a minimum response promises a very strong hand; often with no established trump suit. What will happen next? If partner has a terrible hand, he is expected to bid 2♠. Any other bid by him promises some values. If he rebids 2♡ or 2NT or 3♠, you will raise. If all he can do is bid 2♠, you should pass and hope to go plus.

Rebids by the Takeout Doubler

	North	
Contract: 4♡	♠ A 7 4 2	
Lead: ◊4	♡ Q 3 2	
Neither side vul	◊ 10 9 7	
	♣ 10 5 3	

South
♠ K 6 3
♡ A K J 10 9
◊ A
♣ A 7 6 4

West	North	East	South
—	—	1◊	Dbl
Pass	1♠	Pass	2♡
Pass	3♡	Pass	4♡
All Pass			

On the opening lead, East follows with the ◊K and you win your ◊A.

Question 1: How many losers do you have?

Question 2: Should you draw trumps now?

Question 3: How can you make the hand if neither black suit divides 3-3?

Question 1: How many losers do you have?

Answer: In addition to one spade loser, you could lose three club tricks.

Question 2: Should you draw trumps now?

Answer: Absolutely not!

Question 3: How can you make the hand if neither black suit divides 3-3?

Answer: The key is to ruff your last club with dummy's ♡Q. Once you cash your spade and club winners and continue with clubs, no defense can stop you. I would play as follows:

Trick 2: Lead a spade to dummy's ace.
Trick 3: Lead a spade to your king.
Trick 4: Cash the ♣A.
Trick 5: Concede a club trick. East will win.
Trick 6: Assume East returns a trump. Win the ♡A.
Trick 7: Concede a club trick. West will win.
Trick 8: Assume West returns a trump. Win the ♡K.
Trick 9: Ruff your last club with dummy's ♡Q.

You now have seven tricks, and still have three trump winners in your hand. Making four.

Rebids by the Takeout Doubler

Here is the entire deal:

North

Contract: 4♡
Lead: ◇4
Neither side vul

♠ A 7 4 2
♡ Q 3 2
◇ 10 9 7
♣ 10 5 3

West	*East*
♠ 10 8	♠ Q J 9 5
♡ 6 5 4	♡ 8 7
◇ Q 8 6 4	◇ K J 5 3 2
♣ J 9 8 2	♣ K Q

South
♠ K 6 3
♡ A K J 10 9
◇ A
♣ A 7 6 4

West	North	East	South
—	—	1◇	Dbl
Pass	1♠	Pass	2♡
Pass	3♡	Pass	4♡
All Pass			

West	North	East	South
3♡	Pass	Pass	???

You try hard to be aggressive in the balancing seat, but at this level, some discretion is needed. HCP are relevant, as is vulnerability, but distribution is even more important.

When you have a borderline hand, the key is your holding in the opponent's suit. The shorter you are, the harder you should try to compete.

Once East has passed, it is reasonable to expect your partner to have some of the missing high cards. Of course, East's pass did not deny a strong hand. East may have passed a good hand that was not quite strong enough for game after West's weak bid.

When the opponents stop bidding below game, your side must have some strength. If you have a modest hand, partner must have some high cards. Therefore, if you have a shapely hand but you're not blessed with a lot of HCP, be eager to compete.

The next three pages contain a list of options for the player in the balancing seat. Each category includes two examples. The first one is straightforward, followed by a less-than-obvious example.

Balancing After LHO Preempts

West	North	East	South
3♡	Pass	Pass	???

Pass: In addition to weak hands, you also should pass reasonable hands when you have no good option, usually based on the wrong distribution.

♠ Q 4 3 ♡ J 7 5 ◇ K Q 9 8 6 ♣ K 5

♠ A ♡ 8 7 5 4 ◇ K Q 8 2 ♣ A Q 6 4

Double: Because it is the most flexible call, you should be eager to double whenever possible. A takeout double gives partner a chance to pass for penalties with a suitable hand, as well as preserving the opportunity to play in 3NT. Accordingly, you should be willing to double with imperfect distribution, such as a hand that contains a long minor suit.

♠ A 10 8 7 ♡ 6 ◇ A Q 9 8 ♣ J 5 4 3

♠ 7 6 4 ♡ 4 ◇ A Q 7 ♣ A K J 7 6 4

3♠: There are several reasons to justify this balancing action with many hands. Showing the unbid major is always a high priority, and bidding your suit at the same level as the opponents' is equally desirable. Therefore, the minimum needed for this bid is *much* lower than what is needed to balance with 4♣ or 4◇.

♠ A Q 8 6 5 3 ♡ 6 3 ◇ A J 7 5 ♣ 4

♠ Q J 10 9 7 ♡ — ◇ 8 5 4 ♣ A 10 9 7 5

3NT: This is *definitely* the contract of choice after an enemy preempt. Not only is it the cheapest game, but enemy ruffs and bad trump splits are no longer a concern. Also, remember that the preemptor usually lacks an outside entry.
If your side has a stopper you will often be able to isolate the preemptor and play "2 against 1" against his partner. This is especially true with a holding such as Ax or Axx in the preemptor's suit, which allows you to hold up if need be.

♠ K 7 ♡ K J 6 ♢ K Q J 9 5 ♣ A 8 5
♠ Q 2 ♡ A 9 ♢ A Q J 9 7 6 5 ♣ 9 5

4♣ or 4♢: Because you are giving up on 3NT, you should not be eager to overcall four of a minor. The only hands that qualify are ones with *very* unbalanced distribution.

♠ Q 5 ♡ — ♢ A Q 7 4 ♣ K J 10 7 6 5 3
♠ K J 10 3 ♡ 8 ♢ K J 9 7 6 4 3 ♣ 6

4♡: At this level, a Michaels Cue-Bid promises a good hand with five spades and a 5-card or 6-card minor. If partner does not like spades, he can bid 4NT to ask for your minor.

♠ K Q 8 7 5 ♡ A 7 ♢ — ♣ K J 8 7 6 4
♠ A Q 10 9 6 ♡ — ♢ A Q 9 8 4 ♣ 9 8 5

Jump to 4♠: You can't "preempt a preempt," so this jump shows a very strong hand with a long, strong suit.

♠ K Q 9 8 7 5 4　♡ A Q　◇ 8　♣ K Q 9

♠ A K J 8 6 2　♡ 7　◇ 9 7　♣ A K J 9

Jump to 4NT: *This* Unusual Notrump overcall promises a very good hand with great length in the minors, often 6-5.

♠ 7 6　♡ —　◇ A Q J 10 7　♣ A Q 9 8 6 4

♠ 7　♡ —　◇ K J 9 7 6 4　♣ A 10 9 8 5 3

Jump to 5♣ or 5◇: This strong jump-overcall is based on an independent suit and enough playing strength to justify contracting for 11 tricks. If partner happens to have strength, he's more than welcome to raise.

♠ K Q　♡ —　◇ K J 9　♣ A K Q 9 8 6 5 3

♠ A　♡ 6　◇ K Q J 9 7 6 5 4 2　♣ A Q

By the way: The meaning of all the bids on pages 52-54 is the same if your RHO preempts and you are in the direct seat. However, in that case, the minimum strength needed to make these bids is a little greater than if you're in the balancing seat.

Balancing After LHO Preempts

On each of these hands, the auction has begun:

West	North	East	South
3♡	Pass	Pass	???

As South, evaluate each hand and decide what to do. Neither side is vulnerable.

1. ♠ A ♡ A Q 9 ◇ J 7 5 4 2 ♣ A J 10 8

2. ♠ A 10 9 ♡ 9 ◇ A K J 9 8 6 ♣ K J 5

3. ♠ K Q 9 7 5 4 ♡ 5 ◇ 8 4 ♣ K J 10 7

4. ♠ Q ♡ 8 6 4 ◇ Q 9 6 5 4 2 ♣ A K J

5. ♠ A Q J 10 9 7 ♡ — ◇ A 10 8 6 5 ♣ 9 4

6. ♠ K 6 ♡ K J 8 ◇ 7 5 ♣ A K Q J 7 5

7. ♠ A 6 ♡ A 8 ◇ A Q J 10 8 ♣ 7 5 4 3

8. ♠ 7 5 ♡ — ◇ A Q 10 9 8 ♣ K Q 9 6 4 3

9. ♠ A Q 10 9 8 ♡ — ◇ 7 5 ♣ K Q 9 6 4 3

10. ♠ A Q 10 ♡ 8 ◇ 8 ♣ A K J 10 8 6 5 2

West	*North*	*East*	*South*
3♡	Pass	Pass	???

1.   ♠ A   ♡ A Q 9   ◇ J 7 5 4 2   ♣ A J 10 8

Bid 3NT. Not a perfect hand for the bid, but West's preempt left you with very little room to maneuver. Consider the alternatives:

Pass: Not very enterprising with the best hand at the table.

Double: Out of the question with a singleton spade.

4◇:   Not only do you have a lousy suit, but you'll bypass your most likely game (3NT).

2.   ♠ A 10 9   ♡ 9   ◇ A K J 9 8 6   ♣ K J 5

Double. Much more flexible than bidding 4◇. There is nothing wrong with *this* diamond suit, but, if you overcall in diamonds, you're giving up on 3NT (or defending 3♡ doubled). If partner responds to your double with a bid of 3♠ or 4♣, you'll bid 4◇ and hope for the best.

3.   ♠ K Q 9 7 5 4   ♡ 5   ◇ 8 4   ♣ K J 10 7

Bid 3♠. Once East fails to respond to West's preempt and you have only 9 HCP, you can be sure that your partner has at least a fair hand. Not only do you have attractive 6-4 distribution, but all your honors and intermediates are concentrated in your two long suits, which makes this balancing bid clear-cut.

4. ♠ Q   ♡ 8 6 4   ◇ Q 9 6 5 4 2   ♣ A K J
Pass. You try to be aggressive in the balancing seat,
but bidding 4◇ here is going too far. If you had a
singleton heart, or if you could show your long suit at
the three level, you'd be willing to take some action.

5. ♠ A Q J 10 9 7   ♡ —   ◇ A 10 8 6 5   ♣ 9 4
Bid 4♠, promising a hand too strong to overcall 3♠.
With your spectacular offensive hand, you can't risk
ending up in a part score. If it is correct to bid 3♠
with example #3, it can't be right to make the same
bid with *this* hand. Because of your *independent
major suit*, you are willing to ignore your diamonds
and not bother with a Michaels Cue-Bid.

6. ♠ K 6   ♡ K J 8   ◇ 7 5   ♣ A K Q J 7 5
Bid 3NT, rather than 4♣. As usual, 9 tricks should be
much easier than 11. Your great club suit will come in
handy in 3NT. Don't worry about a sneak attack in
diamonds – you can't play scared bridge.

7. ♠ A 6   ♡ A 8   ◇ A Q J 10 8   ♣ 7 5 4 3
Bid 3NT. Another opportunity to bid the cheapest
game. Because West probably has no outside entry,
your ♡Ax is an ideal holding for 3NT. You expect to
isolate West's hearts by ducking the opening heart lead
and winning the second, which will allow you to play
"2 against 1" against East.

West	North	East	South
3♡	Pass	Pass	???

8. ♠ 7 5   ♡ —   ◇ A Q 10 9 8   ♣ K Q 9 6 4 3

Bid 4NT, which promises both minor suits.
An Unusual Notrump overcall of 4NT is rare, but it
does represent the logical way to show clubs and
diamonds in one breath. With this hand, you don't
need much from partner to score up five of a minor.
A void in the opponent's suit is offensive magic.

9. ♠ A Q 10 9 8   ♡ —   ◇ 7 5   ♣ K Q 9 6 4 3

Make a Michaels Cue-Bid of 4♡, promising spades
plus one of the minors. 6-5-2-0 hands don't grow on
trees; when you have a hand like this, you'd better
make the most of your opportunity. If partner doesn't
like spades, he will bid 4NT to ask for your minor.

10. ♠ A Q 10   ♡ 8   ◇ 8   ♣ A K J 10 8 6 5 2

Bid 5♣. This hand is much too good to balance
with 4♣. Even if partner's only useful card is the ♠K,
your spades and clubs provide an excellent chance
of winning 11 tricks.

Balancing After LHO Preempts

	North		
Contract: 3♡ Dbl	♠ K Q J 5		
Lead: ♠10	♡ —		
Neither side vul	◇ A K 7 5 4		
	♣ J 9 4 2		

East (You)
♠ A 7 6 4
♡ 4 3
◇ Q J 10 8 3
♣ K Q

West	North	East	South
—	—	—	3♡
Pass	Pass	Dbl	All Pass

As East, you choose to make a light, balancing double. When partner leaves it in, you are far from sure that you've done the right thing. Your confidence does not increase when the dummy comes down and you see North's wealth of high cards.

You capture dummy's ♠J with your ♠A.

Question 1: What is your plan to defeat the contract?

Question 2: What should you lead at trick 2?

Question 1: What is your plan to defeat the contract?

Answer: With dummy's imposing spades and diamonds, there's no hope for any additional tricks in those suits. Partner must have a heart trick or two, but the rest will have to come from clubs.

You need to find partner with the ♣A to have any chance of defeating the contract. If declarer has exactly two clubs, you'll take your two club tricks and hope that partner can win two trump tricks.

If declarer has 3-4 clubs, the defense is entitled to three club tricks. But, if you win both your club honors, cashing partner's ♣A won't be easy. You'll try to reach partner by leading a heart, but if South has the ace, he'll win the ♡A and get to the board and discard his remaining club(s) on dummy's winners.

Question 2: What should you lead at trick 2?

Answer: You should lead the ♣Q! **"Unusual situations require unusual solutions."** When your queen wins the trick, it will be obvious to partner that you have the ♣K. When you continue with that card, he'll know that you must have a reason to make such a strange lead. The only possible explanation is that you are trying to tell him that you have a doubleton. He should overtake your ♣K, give you a ruff and wait to score his ♡K for a nervous, but well-deserved +100.

Here is the entire deal:

North

Contract: 3♡ Dbl
Lead: ♠10
Neither side vul

♠ K Q J 5
♡ —
◇ A K 7 5 4
♣ J 9 4 2

West	East (You)
♠ 10 9 8	♠ A 7 6 4
♡ K 9 8 7	♡ 4 3
◇ 9 6 2	◇ Q J 10 8 3
♣ A 10 5	♣ K Q

South

♠ 3 2
♡ A Q J 10 6 5 2
◇ —
♣ 8 7 6 3

West	North	East	South
—	—	—	3♡
Pass	Pass	Dbl	All Pass

61

Chapter 1 - Making the First Move

Page #

11 Most hands worth an opening bid have at least 2 quick tricks. However, no hard and fast rule is possible. You *should* open *some* hands that have 1-1½ quick tricks.

12 Be wary of hands with more queens and jacks than aces and kings, and hands which lack intermediates.

12 I love hands which have all their honors and intermediates concentrated in the two longest suits.

13 On many hands, the advantages of opening 1NT with two doubletons far outweigh the disadvantages. 1NT immediately defines your strength and avoids potential rebid problems.

13 You won't pick up many 6-5 hands, so make the most of every one of them.

14 Three aces should be evaluated as the equivalent of 13 HCP.

14 Preempting with a very weak 4-card major on the side doesn't bother me a bit.

Chapter 2 - After You Open in 3rd Seat

Chapter 3 - After Opener Rebids His Minor

Chapter 4 - Rebids by the Takeout Doubler

Page #

39 After partner forces you to bid by making a takeout double, a non-jump response in a suit shows 0-8 points. With a better hand, you can jump in your suit or cue-bid.

39 When partner makes a weak response to your double, you should pass whenever you believe that game is out of the question. Therefore, *any* bid promises a strong hand.

40 Double followed by 1NT shows 19-20 HCP.

41 If you double and cue-bid after a minimum response, you need a terrific hand, usually 19+ HCP. The cue-bid is forcing for one round, and has no upper limit.

44 KQ doubleton in the opponent's suit is definitely *not* worth 5 HCP.

44 Once you have doubled, you should not raise with only 3-card support.

46 When playing in a suit contract, the difference between 5-4-3-1 distribution and 5-3-3-2 is *very* significant.

45 After a minimum response, a jump-shift by the takeout doubler is not forcing, but is *highly* invitational.

Chapter 5 - Balancing After LHO Preempts

GLOSSARY PLUS

100 honors – pages 27, 34, 64
Refers to a suit which contains 4 of the top 5 cards.

"2 against 1" – pages 53, 57
When one defender can never obtain the lead, or contribute to the defense in any way, declarer and dummy can gang up on the other defender.

Balancing Seat (Pass-out Seat) – page 51, 57, 66
A pass by you would end the auction. Therefore, you try hard to *take some action* rather than allow the enemy to play in a low-level contract.

Cue-Bids after a Takeout Double – Forcing for 1 Round

1. **By the Partner of the Doubler** – pages 39, 43, 65
   This shows at least 12 points.

2. **By the Doubler** – pages 40-42, 46, 65
   This is usually based on a hand with at least 19 HCP.

Direct Seat – page 54
Your RHO did not pass. Because he took action, partner will still get a chance to bid even if you pass.

Fit – pages 20, 21, 27, 29, 32, 33, 63
A term referring to the partnership's combined assets, often with respect to a suit, usually trump. A *good* fit consists of a combined holding of at least eight cards.

Intermediates – appears throughout the book
Tens and nines (and even eights).

Independent Suit – pages 30, 42, 54, 57, 66
A suit that is so long and strong, it doesn't need support.

Michaels Cue-Bid – pages 53, 57, 58, 66
An overcall in the enemy suit that shows at least 5 cards in 2 other suits. The emphasis is on the unbid major(s).

Misfit – pages 28, 32, 34, 64
Describes a deal where each member of a partnership lacks support for his partner's long suit(s).

Playing Tricks – page 14
The number of tricks you expect to win in your own hand. This is only relevant when you have a long, strong suit and become declarer.

Quacks – pages 12, 13, 32
Queens and jacks.

Reverse – pages 13, 21, 63
After a 1-level response, opener's rebid at the two level in a higher-ranking suit than his first bid shows at least 17 points and promises five or six cards in his first suit.

Splinter Bid – pages 22, 29, 30, 42.
A jump into a short suit (0-1 card), promising a fit and values for game (or slam).

Unusual Notrump Overcall – pages 54, 58
A method of showing length in the two lowest unbid suits after an opponent opens.

HIGHLY RECOMMENDED

Future Bridge Cruises with Marty Bergen and Larry Cohen

For more information, call 1-800-367-9980

Hardcover Books by Marty Bergen

More Declarer Play the Bergen Way How to Make More Contracts	$18.95
Declarer Play the Bergen Way 2005 Bridge Book of the Year!	$18.95
Bergen for the Defense Sharpen Your Defensive Skills	$18.95
POINTS SCHMOINTS! All-time Bestseller and Bridge Book of the Year	$19.95
More POINTS SCHMOINTS! Sequel to the Award-Winning Bestseller	$19.95
MARTY SEZ... **Volumes 1, 2, & 3**	$17.95 each

•• VERY SPECIAL OFFER ••

Buy one of these hardcover books from Marty
and receive a **free** copy of any one
of his eight most recent softcover books.
Or, buy 2 hardcovers and get 3 free softcovers!
For a list of softcover books, see next page.
Personalized autographs available upon request.

69

Highly Recommended

Softcover Books by Marty Bergen

Buy 2, then get 1 (equal or lesser price) for half price

Bergen's Best Bridge Tips	$7.95
Bergen's Best Bridge Quizzes, Vol. 1	$7.95
To Open or Not to Open	$6.95
Better Rebidding with Bergen	$7.95
Understanding 1NT Forcing	$5.95
Hand Evaluation: Points, Schmoints!	$7.95
Introduction to Negative Doubles	$6.95
Negative Doubles	$9.95

Better Bidding With Bergen -
Volume 1: Uncontested Auctions	$11.95
Volume 2: Competitive Bidding	$11.95

Interactive CDs by Larry Cohen

Free demos available at:
http://www.larryco.com/DFav52.htm

Play Bridge With Larry Cohen

An exciting opportunity to play question-and-answer with a 21-time national champion. "One of the best products to come along in years. Easy-to-use. Suitable for all players..."

Special Sale!!

Day 1	voted best software 2002	~~$29.95~~	$19
Day 2		~~$29.95~~	$19
Day 3		~~$29.95~~	$19
My Favorite 52	best software 2005	~~$29.95~~	$19

71

CDs by Kit Woolsey - Special sale!

Cavendish 2000:

Day 1	~~$29.95~~	$19
Days 2-3	~~$29.95~~	$19

Books by Larry Cohen

To Bid or Not to Bid - The Law of Total Tricks	$12.95
Following the Law - The Total Tricks Sequel	$12.95

Books by Eddie Kantar

A Treasury of Bridge Bidding Tips	$12.95
Take Your Tricks (Declarer Play)	$12.95
Defensive Tips for Bad Card Holders	$12.95

Special Discount!

365 Bridge Hands with Expert Analysis ~~$13.95~~ only $5

ORDERING INFORMATION

To place your order, call Marty toll-free at:

1-800-386-7432

All major credit cards are welcome.

•• FREE SHIPPING ON ALL SOFTWARE ••
(in the U.S.) if you mention this book

Or send a check or money order (U.S. funds) to:

Marty Bergen
9 River Chase Terrace
Palm Beach Gardens, FL 33418-6817

Please include $3.50 (S&H) for each order.